Colloquial Uzbek

A Mini Course

Kurtuluş Öztopçu

Visiting Assistant Professor
Department of Near Eastern Studies
University of California Berkeley

AUDIO-FORUM
THE LANGUAGE SOURCE

Madison, Connecticut

An Audio Program

Especially created to accompany
this book are 4 instructional
audio cds or 2 audio cassettes.
They are available from the
publisher.

COLLOQUIAL UZBEK

ISBN 1-57970-217-1 Text and Cds
       0-88432-743-4 Text and Cassettes
       0-88432-744-2 Text

This edition published by AudioForum,
One Orchard Park Road, Madison, CT 06443 USA
www.audioforum.com

Printed in the United States of America.

To Korgün and Letafet Öztopçu

Contents

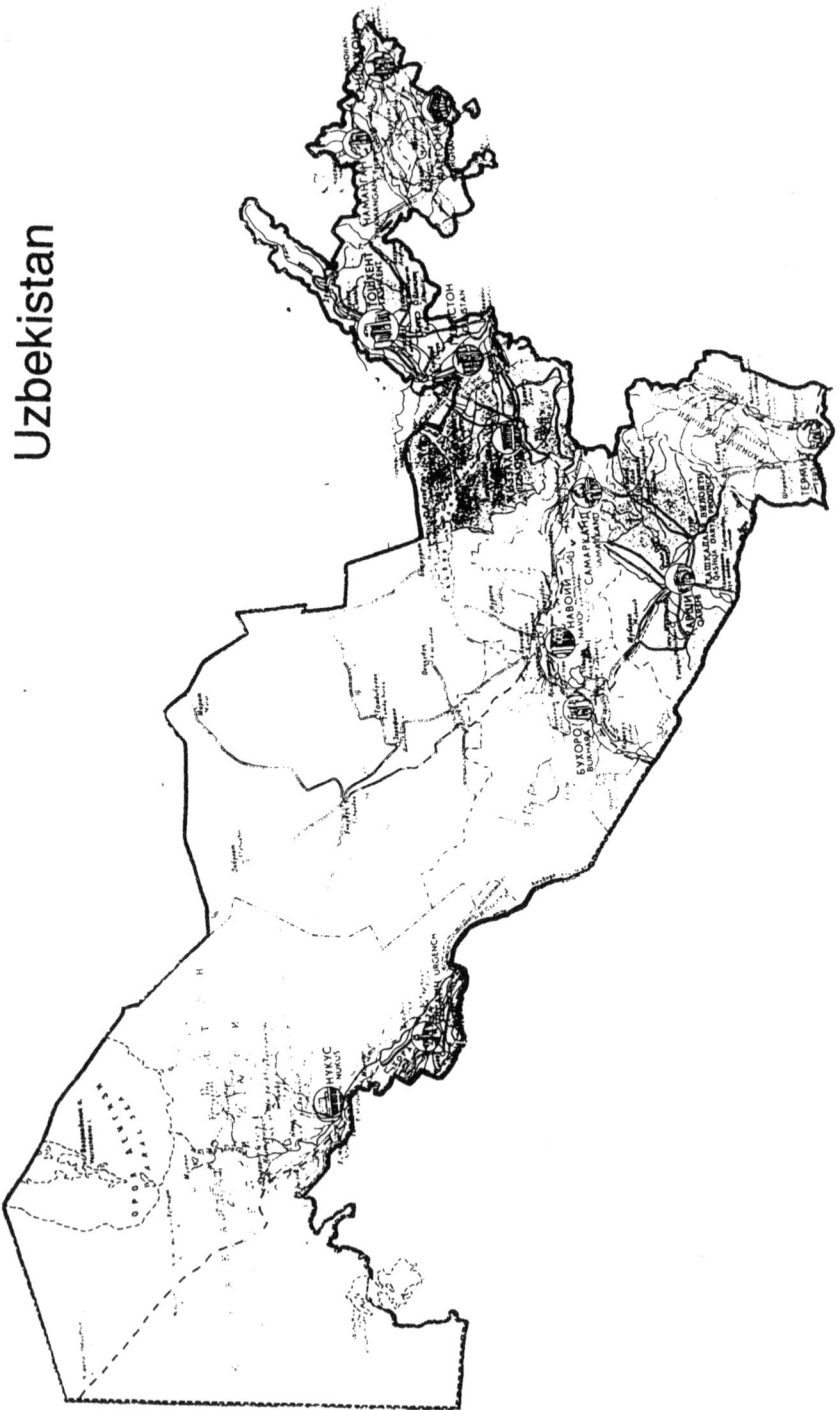

Uzbekistan

Uzbekistan: A Background Note

THE REPUBLIC OF UZBEKISTAN was established on September 1, 1991, after the disintegration of the Soviet Union. Now a full and equal member of the United Nations, the Republic of Uzbekistan has been recognized as a sovereign state by 120 countries, and has diplomatic relations with 45 of them.

GEOGRAPHY: Uzbekistan is situated in the center of the Asian continent between the Amu Darya and Syr Darya rivers. It is bounded by Kazakhstan in the north, Kirgizistan and Tajikistan in the east, Afghanistan in the south, and Turkmenistan in the west. The total land area is 447,400 square kilometers, much of which is occupied by the Kyzylkum Desert. The fertile Fergana valley is situated in the eastern most end of the country. The climate is continental. Winters are cold (January mean temperature is 28 F) and summers, hot (July mean temperature is 80 F). Rainfall is light in the lowlands (3 to 4 inches), however higher in the mountains (24 inches).

POPULATION: 21.5 million

LANGUAGE: Uzbek is the official language of the newly independent Republic of Uzbekistan and is spoken by about 20 million people not only in Uzbekistan but also by Uzbek minorities in neighboring countries such as Tajikistan, Kazakhstan and Kirghizia. Due to its linguistically central position among the Central Asian Turkic languages, Uzbek may also serve as a lingua franca with speakers of Uighur, Kazakh, Kirghiz and Turkmen. Uzbek is one of about 15 modern languages that make up the Turkic Language Family of which the best known member is Turkish. These languages are spoken from the Adriatic Sea in the west to the Altai mountains in the east.

The Uzbek language has a long history dating back to the 8th century AD. Old Uzbek or Chaghatai, which flourished roughly between the thirteenth and nineteenth centuries, left us a remarkably rich literature. Modern Uzbek, which began to assume its present form in the first decades of this century, has been extending this rich heritage. Written in the Arabic alphabet until the end of the 1920s and then in the Latin script for a brief period, Uzbek began to be written in a modified Cyrillic alphabet in 1940-41. Following the disintegration of the Soviet Union, Uzbekistan became an independent state in 1991 and gained immediate importance due to its geopolitical location, rich natural resources and vast potential for business opportunities. Thus today it became ever more important to learn the Uzbek language.

RELIGION: Mostly Sunni Islam

ADMINISTRATION: The Republic of Uzbekistan consists of 12 provinces and includes the Republic of Karakalpakistan. The capital is Tashkent (pop. 2.2 million).

ECONOMY:
Agriculture: Uzbekistan's most important product is cotton. Other products include silk cocoons, karakul pelts, corn, raisins and apricots.
Industries: Machine-building, mining, and chemical industries.
Minerals: Coal, gold, oil, gas, copper, lead, and zinc.

How to Use This Course

Colloquial Uzbek is designed to fulfill the basic communication needs of those who wish to communicate in an Uzbek speaking environment. Since it is a communication/survival based course, its goal is to give the user certain structures along with a sufficient amount of vocabulary to be used to communicate with Uzbek speakers and in certain situations that the user will encounter when (s)he is traveling in Uzbekistan. Long grammatical explanations are avoided, however the mastery of this course will also give the user a sense of the basic Uzbek grammar upon which one can build his/her knowledge to study the language and literature of the Uzbeks.

Uzbek is an agglutinating language, that is to say new words are obtained by adding suffixes (and occasionally non-Uzbek prefixes) to the roots or stems of words. Some other important features of Uzbek include the following: absence of gender and the definite article, absence of duality in nouns and verbal forms, use of postpositions instead of prepositions, inflection of nouns for case, subject object verb syntax, modifiers preceding the modified head nouns, and passive, causative, reflexive, reciprocal and negative forms obtained by suffixes that are added to the verb.

This course consists of 15 chapters and 3 audio cassettes. Two cassettes cover the course given in the book and one cassette contains pronunciation and grammar/situational based drills. There is no specific order to be followed. It is however a good idea first to begin mastering certain portions such as common phrases, frequently used questions, personal and demonstrative pronouns, and numbers etc. because most other sections will require the use of some of this information. The user, through situational dialogues, is given a wide variety of more frequently used sentence structures such as nominal sentences, there is/are sentences, and some of the commonly used verbal sentences. Mastery of this information will give the user a basis for reproducing an infinite number of similar structures as (s)he expands his/her vocabulary.

Materials on cassettes may be used separately or together with the book. The user may listen to the cassettes by using a walkman-type cassette player any time or anywhere (s)he wishes to. Reference cards are prepared to give the user easy and convenient access to the most frequently needed questions, requests, phrases and vocabulary; they could conveniently be used in probably any environment.

One last piece of advise to the user of this or any other language course. When learning a new language it is better to study it as frequently as possible. So it is better to spend 20 minutes studying it every day rather than two or three hours once a week. Try to use your newly acquired knowledge whenever the opportunity arises.

Chapter 1.   Pronunciation

Uzbek is written in a modified Cyrillic script. One character may have more than one sound, and different characters may have the same sound. In the column 'Uzbek Transcription' below, only specific sounds are indicated regardless of their representations in the Uzbek alphabet.

This chart will give the user a general idea of the Uzbek sounds. It is better not to spend too much time on this unit. The user will gain expertise in Uzbek pronunciation by listening to and repeating the words and sentences in the following chapters.

Uzbek Transcription	English Equivalent	Examples	Meaning
a	(1) father	qarash	view
	(2) bad	agar	if
á	qualm	bála	child
b	book	bágh	garden
d	door	dars	lesson
e	pen	men	I
f	find	fan	science
g	goat	gap	sentence
h	hotel	shahar	city
i	(1) bit	kim	who
	(2) Jackson	qiz	girl
j	jam	jáy	place
k	king	kecha	night
l	lift	kalit	key
m	man	mehmán	guest
n	now	nán	bread

o	row	khop	good
p	pen	pul	money
q	*	qancha	how much
r	red	tirsak	elbow
s	sad	narsa	thing
t	tin	áta	father
u	put	gul	flower
v	veal	va	and
w	well	qáwun	melon
y	yes	báy	rich
z	zero	zarur	necessary
ch	chair	chap	left
dz	pleasure	dzurnal	journal
gh	**	oghil	son
kh	similar to Scottish loch	khána	room
ng	song	keng	wide
sh	sheep	básh	head
ts	sits	tsirk	circus
'	indicates a small pause		

*no English equivalent, uvular voice-less stop
**no English equivalent, velar voiced spirant

Chapter 2. The Most Commonly Used Words and Phrases

Yes	**Ha**	No	**Yoq**
Thank you	**Rahmat**	Thank you very much	**Katta rahmat**
You're welcome (Don't mention it)	**Arzimaydi**		
Please	**Marhamat (qilib)**	Excuse me	**Kechirasiz**
Good	**Yakhshi, sáz**	Very good	**Juda yakhshi, juda sáz**
Not good	**Yakhshi emas**	Bad	**Yámán**
Very bad	**Juda yámán**	Not bad	**Yámán emas**
Very	**Juda, kop**	Very much	**Katta, juda kop**
Little	**Áz**	Very little	**Juda áz**
Much, many	**Kop**	O.K.	**Bopti, Khop**
Certainly	**Albatta**	Maybe	**Ehtimál**
That's right	**Toghri**	Not right	**Nátoghri**
With pleasure	**Bajánidil**	Help	**Yárdam, madad**
I apologize	**Uzr**	I am sorry	**Uzr, kechirasiz**
Possible	**Mumkin**	Impossible	**Námumkin**
Sir/Mr.	**Janáb**	Lady/Mrs.	**Khánim**
I know	**Bilaman**	I don't know	**Bilmayman**
I understand	**Tushunaman**	I don't understand	**Tushunmayman**
I want (it)	**Istayman, kháhlayman**		
I don't want (it)	**Istamayman, kháhlamayman**		
Please repeat	**Marhamat qilib takrárlang**		
Please speak slowly	**Marhamat qilib sekinráq sozlang**		

Chapter 3. Meeting and Greeting People

A. Common Greetings

How do you do!	**Assalámu alaykum!**
How do you do!	**Waalaykum assalám!**
Good morning.	**Salám (khayrli erta).**
Good day.	**Salám (khayrli kun).**
Good afternoon.	**Salám (khayrli kun).**
Good evening.	**Salám (khayrli áqshám).**
Good night.	**Khayrli tun.**
Hi, hello.	**Salám.**
Response to 'Hi, hello'	**Salám.**
Welcome.	**Khush kelibsiz.**
Response to 'welcome'	**Khushwaqt boling.**
How are you?	**Qalaysiz? Yakhshimisiz?**
Thank you, I am fine.	**Rahmat, yakhshiman.**

When an Uzbek meets someone (s)he generally says: salám. The response is also salám. Then (s)he says: yakhshimisiz? This is answered repeating the same question. There are also many other questions inquiring a person's wellbeing, the wellbeing of his/her family members, relatives and business etc. It is appropriate to repeat the same greeting as a response for different greetings that you may hear.

B. How to Address People

When Uzbeks introduce themselves they use both their first names and their surnames. Most first names are either Turkic or Islamic. Most surnames are derived from their father's first name and usually have the Russian endings -ov, -yev (for men) and -ova, -yeva (for women). Since the independence of Uzbekistan, many people have replaced -ov, -yev with the words oghli 'son of,' and -ova, -yeva with qizi 'daughter of.'

4

With Russian ending	With Uzbek endings		
	First name	Father's name	son of
Ergash Umarov	**Ergash**	**Umar**	**oghli**
Sabakhat Abdullayeva	**Sabakhat**	**Abdulla**	**qizi**

Good friends usually address one another with terms of relationship such as **aka** *'older brother,'* **ápa'** *older sister' etc. Those who are older are always respected and addressed accordingly by those who are younger:*

Abdulla aka   **Zaynab ápa**

In polite conversations the words **janáb** *'Mr.' and* **khánim** *'Mrs.' are used with the first names:*

Nádira khánim   **Janáb Erkin**

When addressing someone, titles such as **professir, dámla,'** *prof.,' and* **doktir** *can be used either with the first name or by themselves.*

C. Parting

Goodbye	**Khayr**
Bye-bye	**Khayr**
See you later	**(Yana) korushguncha**
Goodbye (go well)	**Yakhshi báring**
Goodbye (stay well)	**Yakhshi qáling**
O.K. See you	**Khop, khayr**
Have a nice trip	**Áq yol**

D. Introductions

Let's get acquainted. My name is...	**Kelinglar tanishamiz. Mening ismim...**
Meet my wife.	**Turmush ortághim bilan tanishing,**
Mrs. ...,	
this is Mr. ...	**... khánim, bu janáb ...**
I'm pleased to meet you.	**Siz bilan tanishganimdan khursantman.**
I'm pleased to see you.	**Sizni korganimdan khursantman.**

My name is ...	**Ismim ...,**
and this is my friend ...	**bu mening dostim ...**
What's your name?	**Ismingiz nima?**

E. Pronouns

Personal Pronouns

I	**men**
you	**sen**
he, she, it	**u**
we	**biz**
you	**siz**
they	**ular**

*Note that Uzbek has two pronouns for 'you': **sen** for the singular, **siz** for the plural. However **siz** can also be used for the singular in polite speech.*

Verb Suffixes

men bilaman	I know	**biz bilamiz**	we know
sen bilasan	you know	**siz bilasiz**	you know
u biladi	he, she, it knows	**ular biladi(lar)**	they know

*The suffix used for the second person plural, -**siz**, can also be used for the second person singular to indicate politeness along with or without the word **siz**: [**siz**] **bilasiz** means 'you know' either for one person or more than one person. To be polite, it is a good idea to use the second* *person plural forms of pronouns and personal suffixes to address one person.*

Uzbek has also two sets of personal suffixes indicating singular and plural. The set used for the second person plural can also be used for the second person singular to indicate politeness along with the word siz.

Malika khánim <u>meni</u> kordi.	Mrs. Malika saw <u>me</u>.
seni	you
uni	him, her, it
bizni	us
sizni	you
ularni	them

mening kitábim	my book
sening uying	your house
uning radyosi	his, her, its radio
bizning kitábimiz	our book
sizning uyingiz	your house
ularning radyosi	their radio

Again it is better to use the second person plural form to address one person for politeness.

Chapter 4.   Numbers

1-99

1	**bir**	34	ottiz tort	67	áltmish yetti
2	**ikki**	35	ottiz besh	68	áltmish sakkiz
3	**uch**	36	ottiz álti	69	áltmish toqqiz
4	**tort**	37	ottiz yetti	70	**yetmish**
5	**besh**	38	ottiz sakkiz	71	yetmish bir
6	**álti**	39	ottiz toqqiz	72	yetmish ikki
7	**yetti**	40	**qirq**	73	yetmish uch
8	**sakkiz**	41	qirq bir	74	yetmish tort
9	**toqqiz**	42	qirq ikki	75	yetmish besh
10	**on**	43	qirq uch	76	yetmish álti
11	**on bir**	44	qirq tort	77	yetmish yetti
12	**on ikki**	45	qirq besh	78	yetmish sakkiz
13	**on uch**	46	qirq álti	79	yetmish toqqiz
14	**on tort**	47	qirq yetti	80	**saksán**
15	**on besh**	48	qirq sakkiz	81	saksán bir
16	**on álti**	49	qirq toqqiz	82	saksán ikki
17	**on yetti**	50	**ellik**	83	saksán uch
18	**on sakkiz**	51	ellik bir	84	saksán tort
19	**on toqqiz**	52	ellik ikki	85	saksán besh
20	**yigirma**	53	ellik uch	86	saksán álti
21	yigirma bir	54	ellik tort	87	saksán yetti
22	yigirma ikki	55	ellik besh	88	saksán sakkiz
23	yigirma uch	56	ellik álti	89	saksán toqqiz
24	yigirma tort	57	ellik yetti	90	**toqsán**
25	yigirma besh	58	ellik sakkiz	91	toqsán bir
26	yigirma álti	59	ellik toqqiz	92	toqsán ikki
27	yigirma yetti	60	**áltmish**	93	toqsán uch
28	yigirma sakkiz	61	áltmish bir	94	toqsán tort
29	yigirma toqqiz	62	áltmish ikki	95	toqsán besh
30	**ottiz**	63	áltmish uch	96	toqsán álti

31	ottiz bir	64	áltmish tort	97	toqsán yetti
32	ottiz ikki	65	áltmish besh	98	toqsán sakkiz
33	ottiz uch	66	áltmish álti	99	toqsán toqqiz

100s

100	bir yuz	101	bir yuz bir
200	ikki yuz	215	ikki yuz on besh
300	uch yuz	326	uch yuz yigirma álti
400	tort yuz	433	tort yuz ottiz uch
500	besh yuz	547	besh yuz qirq yetti
600	álti yuz	658	álti yuz ellik sakkiz
700	yetti yuz	769	yetti yuz áltmish toqqiz
800	sakkiz yuz	871	sakkiz yuz yetmish bir
900	toqqiz yuz	982	toqqiz yuz saksán ikki

1000s

1,000	bir ming	1,001	bir ming bir
2,000	ikki ming	2,234	ikki ming ikki yuz ottiz tort
3,000	uch ming	3,500	uch ming besh yuz
4,000	tort ming	4,867	tort ming sakkiz yuz áltmish yetti
10,000	on ming	10,500	on ming besh yuz
42,000	qirq ikki ming	25,311	yigirma besh ming uch yuz on bir
700,000	yetti yuz ming	250,300	ikki yuz ellik ming uch yuz

1,000,000

1,000,000	bir milyon	1,500,000	bir milyon besh yuz ming
2,000,000	ikki milyon	2,350,000	ikki milyon uch yuz ellik ming
50,000,000	ellik milyon		

1st, 2nd etc.

1st	birinchi	4th	tortinchi
2nd	ikkinchi	5th	beshinchi
3rd	uchinchi		etc [number + inci]

Fractions, Decimals, and Percentages

one half	**yarim, ikkidan bir**
one quarter	**chárak, torttan bir**
three quarters	**torttan uch**
one third	**uchdan bir**
1.5	**bir yarim**
5.8	**besh butun ondan sakkiz**
7.25	**yetti butun yuzdan yigirma besh**
10%	**on fáiz**
25%	**yigirma besh fáiz**

Chapter 5.   Time

A. Hours, Minutes & Seconds

What time is it now?	**Házir sáat necha?**
(It's) one o'clock.	**Sáat bir.**

sáat means 'time, hour, clock, watch.'

(It's) two o'clock.	**Sáat ikki.**
(It's) three o'clock.	**Sáat uch.**
(It's) half past one.	**Sáat bir yarim.**
(It's) half past eight.	**Sáat sakkiz yarim.**
(It's) a quarter past five.	**Sáat beshdan chárak otti.**
(It's) 5 minutes past four.	**Sáat torttan besh minut otti.**
(It's) quarter to ten.	**Sáat chárak kam on.**
(It's) 20 minutes to seven.	**Sáat yigirma minuti kam yetti.**
At what time?	**Sáat nechada?**
at 7.00 a.m.	**Ertalab sáat yettida.** (morning)
at 1.00 p.m.	**Tushda sáat birda.** (midday)
at 3.00 p.m.	**Tushdan keyin uchda.** (afternoon)
at 6.30 p.m.	**Áqshám sáat álti yarimda.** (evening)
at 11.00 p.m.	**Kechasi sáat on birda.** (night)

When?	**Qachán?**	second	**sekunt**
How long?	**Qancha waqt?**	five minutes	**besh minut**
10 minutes ago.	**on minut áldin**	in two hours	**ikki sáat ichida**
2 hours ago	**ikki sáat áldin**	an hour later	**bir sáattan song**
until five o'clock	**sáat beshgacha**	three hours later	**uch sáattan song**
half an hour	**yarim sáat**	a quarter of an hour	**chárak sáat**
for 30 seconds	**ottiz sekunt**	for 15 minutes	**on besh minut**
for two hours	**ikki sáat**	Do you have time?	**Waqtingiz bármi?**
I have time.	**Waqtim bár.**		
I don't have time.	**Waqtim yoq.**		

B. Days, Months, and Dates

Monday	**dushanba**	Friday	**juma**
Tuesday	**seshanba**	Saturday	**shanba**
Wednesday	**chárshanba**	Sunday	**yakshanba**
Thursday	**payshanba**		

Months

January	**yanvar**	July	**iyul**
February	**fevral**	August	**awgust**
March	**mart**	September	**sentyabr**
April	**aprel**	October	**aktyabr**
May	**may**	November	**nayabr**
June	**iyun**	December	**dekabr**

the 13th of May	**Mayning on uchu**
1993	**Bir ming toqqiz yuz toqsán uch**
In May 1980	**Bir ming toqqiz yuz saksáninchi yili may áyida**
What's the date today?	**Bugun nechanchi chislo?**
Today is the 5th of April.	**Bugun beshinchi aprel.**
What day is it today?	**Bugun qaysi kun?**
Today is Monday.	**Bugun dushanba.**

day	**kun**	month	**áy**
today	**bugun**	this month	**bu áy**
tomorrow	**ertaga**	next month	**kelasi áy**

the day after tomorrow	**indinga**	last month	**otgan áyda**
yesterday	**kecha**	every month	**har áyda**
everyday	**har kuni**	year	**yil**
week	**hafta**	this year	**bu yil**
this week	**shu haftada**	next year	**kelasi yil**
next week	**kelasi hafta**	last year	**otgan yili**
last week	**otgan haftada**	every Friday	**har juma**

Chapter 6.   Personal Information

A. Vocabulary

age/old	**yásh**	to be born	**tughil-**
big	**katta**	birthday	**tughilgan kun**
boy	**oghil**	children	**bálalar**
doctor	**doktir**	engineer	**endzenyer**
family	**áila**	girl	**qiz**
to graduate	**tugat-***	husband	**er**
man	**erkak**	name	**isim**
to marry	**uylan-**	nationality	**millat**
occupation	**kasb**	person	**kishi**
school	**maktab**	single	**boydáq**
surname	**familiya**	teacher	**oqituwchi**
wife	**khátin**	woman	**ayál**
to work	**ishla-**	year	**yil**

*dash sign after verbs indicates the infinitive form of the verb which is -**máq** in Uzbek.

B. Key Questions and Phrases

Name

What is your name?	**Ismingiz nima?**
My name is...	**Ismim ...**
What is your surname?	**Familiyangiz nima?**
My surname is...	**Familiyam ...**
What is your wife's name?	**Khátiningizning ismi nima?**
My wife's name is...	**Khátinimning ismi ...**
What is your husband's name?	**Eringizning ismi nima?**
My husband's name is...	**Erimning ismi ...**
What is that person's name?	**Bu kishining ismi nima?**
That person's name is...	**Bu kishining ismi ...**

Age

How old are you?	**Yáshingiz nechada?**
I am 25 years old.	**Men 25 (yigirma besh) yáshdaman.**
How old is that person?	**Bu kishi necha yáshda?**
(S)he is 32 years old.	**U 32 (ottiz ikki) yáshda.**
In what year were you born?	**Siz nechanchi yilda tughilgansiz?**
I was born in 1970.	**Men 1970 yilda tughilganman.**
When is your birthday?	**Sizning tughilgan kuningiz qachán?**
My birthday is May 10th.	**Mening tughilgan kunim oninchi may.**

Family

Are you married? (for a man only)	**Siz uylanganmisiz?**
Are you married? (for a woman only)	**Siz turmushga chiqqanmisiz?**
Yes, I'm married. (for a man only)	**Ha, men uylanganman.**
No, I'm not married. (for a man only)	**Yoq, men uylanmaganman.**
Yes, I'm married. (for a woman only)	**Ha, men turmushga chiqqanman.**
No, I'm not married. (for a woman only)	**Yoq, men turmushga chiqmaganman.**
I'm single. (for a man only)	**Men boydáqman.**
Is your family big?	**Áilangiz kattami?**
Do you have any children?	**Bálalaringiz bármi?**

Nationality

What is your nationality?	**Millatingiz nima?**
I'm an American.	**Men amerikalikman.**
Are you a Russian?	**Siz Orismisiz?**
No, I'm an Uzbek.	**Yoq, men Ozbekman.**

Occupation

What is your occupation?	**Kasbingiz nima?**
I'm an engineer.	**Men endzenyerman.**
I'm a doctor.	**Men doktirman.**
Are you a teacher?	**Siz oqituwchimisiz?**
Yes, I'm a teacher.	**Ha, men oqituwchiman.**
Where do you work?	**Siz qayerda ishlaysiz?**

Education:

Which school did you graduate from?	**Qayerni tugattingiz?**
I graduated from university ...	**Men universitetni tugattim.**

C. Model dialog

What is your name?	**Ismingiz nima?**
My name is ...	**Ismim ...**
What is your surname?	**Familiyangiz nima?**
My surname is ...	**Familiyam ...**
Are you married?	**Siz uylanganmisiz?**
Yes, I am married.	**Ha, men uylanganman.**
Do you have children?	**Bálalaringiz bármi?**
Yes I have a boy and a girl.	**Ha, bir oghlim va bir qizim bár.**
How old are they?	**Yáshlari nechada?**
My son is 7 years old,	**Oghlim yetti yáshda,**
and my daughter is 9 years old.	**qizim toqqiz yáshda.**
What is your wife's occupation.	**Khátiningizning kasbi nima?**
She is a linguist.	**U tilshunás.**
Where does she work?	**U qayerda ishlaydi?**
She works at the university.	**U universitetta ishlaydi.**
Is she an American?	**U amerikalikmi?**
No, she's German.	**Yoq, u nyemis.**

Most inhabitants of Uzbekistan are ethnic Uzbeks, but as in other parts of the former Soviet Union, people of many other ethnic backgrounds also live there. Uzbeks are very friendly and talkative. Most speak Russian in addition to their native Uzbek. Some also know Persian, English, or German. Using their language skills, they make friends with foreigners very quickly.

In Tashkent, a modern western style city, people behave similarly to the Europeans, but in the country and in small towns and villages Uzbek norms, similar to those in the Middle East, are observed. There men are not expected to carry out one-on-one conversations with women or invite them out alone.

D. Supplementary Vocabulary

aged	**keksa**	archeologist	**arkhyealog**
architect	**arkhityektor**	brother (older)	**aka**
brother (younger)	**uka**	day	**kun**
Englishman	**ingiliz**	faculty	**fakultyet**
father	**áta**	french	**frantsuz**
German	**nyemis**	grandchild	**nabira**
lecture	**lektsiya**	historian	**tarikhchi**
library	**kutupkhána**	mother	**ána**
month	**áy**	parents	**áta-ána**
professor	**professir**	relative	**qarindásh**
scholarship	**stipendiya**	sister (older)	**ápa**
sister (younger)	**singil**	student	**oquwchi**
to study	**oqi-**	writer	**yázuwchi**
year	**yil**	young	**yásh**

Chapter 7.   Finding Your Way Around

A. Vocabulary

left	**chap**	right	**ong**
north	**shimál**	south	**janup**
east	**sharq**	west	**gharp**
in front (of)	**áldida**	behind	**árqasida**
inside	**ichida**	outside	**tashqarida**
here	**bu yerda**	there	**u yerda**
near	**yaqin**	far	**uzáq, uzun**
underneath	**tagida**	on top (of)	**ustida**
at the end (of)	**ákhirida**	in the middle	**ortasida**
Where?	**qayerda**	between	**árasida**
next to (beside)	**yánida**	by (with)	**bilan**
at, in	**-da**	up to, as far as	**-gacha**
to	**-ga**	from	**-dan**

B. Directions

on the <u>left</u> side of that street	**u kochaning <u>chap</u> támánida**
right	**ong**
Turn <u>left</u>.	**<u>Chapga</u> buriling.**
right	**ongga**
in the <u>northern</u> part of Uzbekistan	**Ozbekistánning <u>shimál</u> qismida**
southern	**janup**
eastern	**sharq**
western	**ghar**
<u>in front of</u> the museum	**muzeyning <u>áldida</u>**
behind	**árqasida**
inside	**ichida**
outside	**tashqarisida**
at the museum	**muzeyda**
Follow this road.	**Shu yoldan ketavering.**

Just go straight ahead.	**Toghri báring.**
You have to go in <u>that</u> direction.	**Siz <u>u</u> tomonga yurishingiz kerak.**
left	**chap**
the opposite	**qarama-qarshi**
<u>50 kilometers</u> from here	**bu yerdan <u>ellik (50) kilometr</u>**
100 meters	**yuz (100) metr**
far	**uzáq**
not far	**uzáq emas**

C. Key Questions and Phrases

Is there a <u>bank</u> near here?	**Bu atráfda <u>bank</u> bármi?**
doctor	**doktir**
hospital	**kasalkhána**
hotel	**mehmánkhána**
pharmacy	**dárikhána**
restaurant	**restoran**
subway station	**metro stantsiyasi**
Where is the <u>police station</u>?	**<u>Militsiya idárasi</u> qayerda?**
cinema	**kinatyeatr**
museum	**muzey**
American Embassy	**amerikan konsulkhánasi**
Post Office	**pochta**
railway station	**vagzal**
zoo	**haywánát bághi**
Where is the nearest <u>bank</u>?	**Eng yaqin <u>bank</u> qayerda?**
bus-stop	**aftobus bekati**
exibition	**korgazma**
hotel	**mehmánkhána**
downtown	**shaharning markazi**
Is the <u>market</u> far from here?	**<u>Bázár</u> bu yerdan uzáqmi?**
university	**universityet**
village	**qishláq**
madrasah	**madrasa**
church	**cherkow**
mosque	**maschit**

How many kilometers from here to..	**Bu yerdan ... necha kilometr?**
Tashkent?	**Táshkengacha**
Samarkand	**Samarqangacha**
Alma-Ata	**Alma-atagacha**
Bukhara	**Bukhárágacha**
How does one get to the	**qanday báriladi?**
Navai Museum?	**Nawáiy muzeyiga**
to the airport	**ayeroportga**
to the Uzbekistan Hotel	**Ozbekistán mehmánkhánasiga**
to Farabi Street	**Fárábiy kochasiga**

Due to the Russian influence of the past hundred years, street signs and place names are written both in Uzbek and Russian.

D. Model Dialog

Excuse me, is there a	**Kechirasiz, bu atráfda**
hotel around here?	**mehmánkhána bármi?**
Yes, there is.	**Ha, bár.**
Behind the Lenin Museum.	**Lenin muzeyining árqasida.**
Thank you very much.	**Sizga katta rahmat.**
You're welcome.	**Arzimaydi.**
Please tell me how	**Marhamat qilib ayting,**
to go to the Navai Street?	**Nawáiy kochasiga qanday báriladi?**
Where would you like to go?	**Siz qayerga bármáqchisiz?**
I would like to go to the Tashkent Hotel.	**Men Táshkent mehmánkhánasiga bármáqchiman.**

It's in the center of the city.	**U shaharning markazida.**
Is it far away from here?	**U bu yerdan uzáqdami?**
It's not that far.	**Uncha uzáq emas.**
How can I go there?	**U yerga qanday bárishim mumkin?**
You can go there on the subway.	**U yerga metro bilan bárishingiz mumkin.**
Where is the nearest subway station?	**Eng yaqin metro stantsiyas i qayerda?**
It is just behind that building.	**Ana u bináning árqasida.**
How much is the fare?	**Yol haqi qancha?**
Two rubles.	**Ikki som.**
Thank you very much	**Katta rahmat.**

E. Supplementary Vocabulary

tram	**tramway**	trolleybus	**traleybus**
on foot	**piyáda**	ticket	**bilet**
monument	**yádgárlik**	old city	**eski shahar**
minaret	**minár**	palace	**saráy**
important sightseeing places		**diqqatga sazávár jáylar**	

Chapter 8. Transportation

A. Types of Transport

car	**mashina**	taxi	**taksi**
train	**poyezd**	plane	**tayyára, samalyot**
ship	**parakhod**	boat	**kema**
yacht	**yahta**	bicycle	**velasiped**
motor-cycle	**mototsikil**	bus	**aftobus**
ferry	**parom**	helicopter	**vertalyot**

B. Dialog: Taxi

I need a taxi.	**Menga taksi kerak.**
Is this taxi free?	**Bu taksi boshmi?**
Can you take me ...	**Meni ... álib bárib qoysangiz?**
to the railway station?	**temir yol stantsiyasiga**
to the airport	**ayeroportga**
downtown	**shaharning markaziga**
Where would you like to go?	**Qayerga bármáqchisiz?**
I want to go ...	**... ketmáqchiman.**
to Pushkin Street.	**Pushkin kochasiga**
to Tashkent Hotel.	**Táshkent mehmánkhánasiga**
Please stop <u>here</u>.	**Marhamat <u>bu yerda</u> tokhtating.**
in front of that building	**u bináning áldida**
Please wait here for me.	**Marhamat bu yerda meni kuting.**
Please go <u>faster</u>.	**Marhamat <u>tezráq</u> haydang.**
slower	**astaráq**
How much do I owe you?	**Sizga qancha tolashim kerak?**

C. Dialog: Train

Excuse me,	**Kechirasiz,**
where is the ticket office?	**bilet kassasi qayerda?**

When is the first train to Samarkand?	Samarqanga birinchi poyezd qachán boladi?
Is there a sleeping car?	Kupeli vagon bármi?
One ticket to Samarkand.	Samarqanga bitta bilet.
two tickets	ikkita
first class ticket	birinchi darajali bilet
second class	ikkinchi darajali
return ticket	bárish kelish bileti
passanger train	passajir poyezdi
express train	ekspres poyezdi
What is the fare to Tashkent?	Táshkentga biletqancha turadi?
How much is the ticket from Tashkent to Bukhara?	Táshkenttan Bukhárágaca bilet qancha turadi?
What time does the train depart?	Poyezd qachán jonaydi?
arrive	keladi
Is this the train to Dushanba?	Dushanbaga ketadigan poyezd bumi?
to Khiva	Khivaga
No, this train is going to Tashkent.	Yoq, bu poyezd Táshkentga báradi.
Yes, this train is going to Khiva.	Ha, bu poyezd Khivaga báradi.
Which platform is ours?	Biz qaysi platformadan ketamiz?
Is this seat taken?	Bu jáy boshmi?
May I open the window?	Derazani áchsam boladimi?
close	yápsam
When do we get to Tashkent?	Táshkentga qachán yetib báramiz?
to Samarkand	Samarqanga
No smoking	Chekilmasin

D. Dialog: Plane

Where is the information?	Sprafka byurosi qayerda?
Is there a plane to Tashkent...	Táshkentga ... samalyot bármi?
tomorrow?	ertalap
on Friday	juma kuni
When is there a flight ...	... samalyot qaysi waqtlarda uchadi?
to Farghana	Farghánága
to Khiva	Khivaga

Where are plane tickets sold?	**Samalyotga bilet qayerda sátiladi?**
How much is a ticket	**Maskvaga bitta bilet**
to Moscow?	**necha pul turadi?**
I need a ticket to Moscow.	**Menga Maskvaga bilet kerak.**
What is the <u>departure</u> time?	**Samalyot sáat nechada <u>uchadi</u>?**
arrival	**keladi?**
What is the flight time?	**Uchish waqti qancha?**
May I smoke?	**Chekish mumkinmi?**
May I unfasten my seat belt?	**Kamarimni boshatsam boladimi?**

Uzbekistan has a very extensive mass transit system. Most people use buses and taxis in the cities. Taxi fares are very low. Tashkent has an excellent subway system in addition to bus, trolleybus, and streetcar lines. The subway is very efficient, clean and cheap. Highways and railways connect almost all cities. The highway between Tashkent and Samarkand is quite good. There is also an air service linking most major cities. It is better to fly between different cities within the country, and it is advisable to have your arrangements made through professional tour agencies.

E. Supplementary Vocabulary

airline	**hawá yoli**	bus terminal	**aftavagzal**
conductor	**kanduktir**	crossing	**chárraha**
flight	**reys**	passenger	**yoláwchi**
pavement	**yolka**	traffic-light	**svetafor**
entrance	**kirish**	exit	**chikish**
baggage	**yuk**	excess baggage	**ártiqcha yuk**
toilet	**tualet**	waiting area	**kutish zali**
flight altitude	**uchish balandligi**	cruising speed	**uchish tezligi**
handbag	**sumka**	suitcase	**chamadán**

Chapter 9.   Health and The Body

A. Parts of the Body

arm	qol	kidney	boyrak
back	árqa	leg	áyáq
body	tan	lip	lab
cheek	yánáq	lung	opka
chest	kokrak	mouth	ághiz
chin	jagh	neck	ensa
ear	quláq	nose	burun
eye	koz	shoulder	yelka
face	yuz	skin	teri
finger	barmáq	size, height	boy
foot	áyáq	stomach	áshqázán
hair	sách	throat	támáq
hand	qol	tongue	til
head	básh	tooth	tish
heart	yurak	waist	bel

B. Feeling Ill

I don't feel well.	**Mening mazam yoq.**
I am sick.	**Men kasalman.**
I have a <u>head</u> ache.	**Mening <u>báshim</u> ághriyapti.**
a stomach	**áshqázánim**
an ear	**qulághim**
a tooth	**tishim**
I have a sore <u>throat</u>.	**Mening <u>támághim</u> ághriyapti.**
back	**árqam**
arm	**qolim**
Please call a doctor.	**Iltimás, doktir chaqiring.**

Please take me <u>to a doctor</u>. Iltimás, meni <u>doktirga</u> álib báring.
   to the hospital kasalkhánaga
   to a policlinic poliklinikaga
Is there a doctor who can speak English? Ingilizcha gapiradigan doktir bármi?

C. At the Doctor's Office

Where does it hurt?	Qayeringiz ághriydi?
Does it hurt if I press here?	Shu yerni básganimda ághriqni sezyapsizmi?
I don't have an appetite.	Ishtaham yoq.
I have a cold.	Shamálladim.
I've had food-poisoning.	Áziq-áwqattan zaharlandim.
I am dizzy.	Báshim aylanyapti.
I'm constipated.	Ichim qatti.
I feel nauseous	Konglim ayniyapti.
I have a fever.	Isitmam bár.
Open your mouth.	Ághzingizni áching.
Say "a, a"	"a, a" deng.
Stick out your tounge.	Tilingizni korsating.
Cough.	Yotaling.
Take a deep breath.	Chuqur nafas áling.
Don't breathe.	Nafas álmang.
Hold your breath.	Nafasingizni chiqarmang.
Strip to the waist.	Belingizgacha yechining.
I am allergic <u>to penicilin</u>	<u>Pensilinga</u> qarshi allergiyam bár.
to that medicine	u dáriga
to milk	sutga
to egg	tukhumga
I am pregnant.	Hámiladárman.
I have diarrhoea.	Ichim otadi.
I have diabetes.	Qand kasaliman.
I have vomitted <u>twice</u>.	<u>Ikki marta</u> qusdim.
once	bir marta
I have a high blood pressure.	Qán básimim baland.
Take this medicine <u>after meals</u>.	Siz bu dárini <u>áwqatdan keyin</u> ichishingiz kerak.
before meals	áwqattan áldin
3 times a day	kuniga uch marta

One pill <u>once</u> a day.	**Tablyetkadan kuniga <u>bir</u> dána**
twice	**ikki**
3 times	**uch**

D. Model Dialog

I am sick.	**Men kasalman**
What seems to be the problem?	**Sizni nima bezáwta qilyapti?**
I have a sore throat.	**Támághim ághriyapti.**
Let me have a look at your throat.	**Támághingizni korsating.**
Let me take your temperature.	**Isitmangizni olchay.**
You have a high temperature.	**Isitmangiz baland.**
Take a deep breath.	**Chuqur nafas áling.**
Hold your breath.	**Nafasingizni chiqarmang.**
What do I have, doctor?	**Nima kasalim bár ekan doktir?**

You have a slight cold.	**Sal shamállapsiz.**
Take this medicine three times a day.	**Bu dárini kuniga uch marta icing.**
Gargle your throat every 3 hours.	**Támághingizni har uch sáatda chayqap turing.**

Uzbekistan has socialized medicine. Until recently all medical facilities were state owned and operated. Now however some private medical establishments have begun to appear. Nevertheless, medical services and equipment are still inadequate or below European and U.S. standards. Medicines are in short supply. For this reason, visitors to Uzbekistan are advised to take their medications with them.

E. Supplementary Vocabulary

medicine	**dári**	burn	**kuyish**
laxative	**surgi**	rash	**táshma**
swelling	**shish**	pain	**ághriq**
to diet	**parhez qil-**	to diagnose	**diagnoz qoy-**
stroke	**falaj**	rheumatism	**revmatizm**
pneumonia	**pnevmoniya**	mumps	**tepki**
malaria	**bezgak**	diptheria	**difteriya**
measles	**qizamiq**	cancer	**rak**
infection	**infektsiya**	ampule	**ampula**
blood	**qán**	bone	**suyak**
breath	**nafas**	abscess	**chipqán**
poison	**zahar**	pharmacy	**dárikhána**
dentist	**tish doktiri**	optometrist	**koz doktiri**
surgeon	**jarráh**	nurse	**hamshira**

Chapter 10.   Food and Drink

A. Key Words and Expressions

to eat	**ye-**	restaurant	**restoran**
food	**áwqat, táam**	coffe-shop	**kafe**
to drink	**ich-**	canteen	**áshkhána**
drink	**ichimlik**	menu	**menyu**
knife	**picháq**	plate	**taryelka**
fork	**vilka**	cup	**piyála**
spoon	**qáshiq**	glass	**stakan**
dish	**lagancha**	tea-pot	**cháynak**
water-jug	**koza**	salt	**tuz**
pepper	**murch**	waiter	**ofitsant**
napkin	**salfyetka**	to order	**buyurtma ber-**
bread	**nán**	rice (cooked)	**paláw**
breakfast	**nánushta**		
lunch	**tushlik**		
dinner	**kechki áwqat**		

What would you like to <u>eat</u>?	**Marhamat, nima <u>yeyishni</u> kháh laysiz?**
drink	**ichishni**
I'd like <u>coffee</u>.	**Men <u>kofe</u> kháhlayman.**
two bottles of beer	**ikki shisha piwá**
a cup of tea	**bir piyála cháy**
Thank you.	**Rahmat.**
Would you like some <u>fish</u>?	**<u>Baliq</u> istaysizmi?**
chicken	**táwuq**
Would you like fish or chicken?	**Siz baliqmi yeysiz yá táwuqmi yeysiz?**
I'd like some fish.	**Men baliq istayman.**
I do not want <u>chicken</u>.	**Men <u>táwuq</u> istamayman.**
anything	**hech narsa**

Would you like some <u>sugar</u>?	**Siz <u>qand</u> kháhlaysizmi?**
milk	**sut**
salt	**tuz**
pepper	**murch**
bread	**nán**
Yes, please.	**Ha, marhamat.**
No, thank you.	**Yoq, rahmat.**
This food is very <u>delicious</u>.	**Bu áwqat juda <u>mazali</u> ekan**
hot (cold)	**issiq**
salty	**tuzli**
cold	**sáwuq**
Are you hungry?	**Qárningiz áchmi?**
Are you thirsty	**Chanqadingizmi?**
I'm hungry.	**Qárnim ách.**
I'm not thirsty.	**Chanqamadim.**

Uzbek cuisine consists of typical Middle Eastern/Central Asian dishes. The most characteristic are listed below. Delicious fruits grown in Uzbekistan are an important part of the Uzbek diet. Their favorite drink is hot tea (black or green). Alcoholic beverages are consumed mostly on special occasions where only males are expected to drink. On these occasions the honored guest makes a short speech, a toast in vodka is drunk, and other speeches and toasts follow. Uzbeks are very hospitable. Any guest in an Uzbek house is offered food and tea without being asked whether (s)he is hungry or not.

B. Meat

meat	**gosht**	chicken	**táwuq**
beef	**mál goshti**	mutton	**qoy goshti**
beef-steak	**bifshteks**	cutlet	**katlyet**
sausage	**sasiska**	schnitzel	**shnitsel**

C. Vegetables

vegetable	**kokat**	garlic	**sarimsáq**
bean	**lawiya**	egg-plant	**baklaján**

onion	**piyáz**	cabbage	**karam**
potato	**kartoshka**	carrot	**sabzi**
cucumber	**bádring**	spinach	**ismaláq**
celery	**selder**	lettuce	**salat**

D. Fruit

fruit	**meva**	apples	**álma**
pears	**nák**	pomegranate	**anár**
melon	**qáwun**	watermelon	**tarwuz**
grapes	**uzum**	apricots	**orik**
cherries	**gilás**	plums	**álhori**
quince	**behi**	strawberries	**qulupnay**
peaches	**shaftáli**	figs	**anjir**
banana	**banan**	oranges	**apelsin**

E. Drink

water	**su**	iced water	**muzli su**
tea	**cháy**	green tea	**kok cháy**
milk	**sut**	lemonade	**limonad**
juice	**sharbat**	apple juice	**álma sharbati**
grape juice	**uzum sharbati**	tomato juice	**tomat sharbati**
mineral water	**mineral su**	soft drinks	**spirtsiz ichimliklar**
vodka	**araq**	beer	**piwá**
wine	**musallas**	sweet wine	**shirin musallas**
champagne	**shampan vinasi**	cognac	**kanyak**

F. Uzbek National Food

chuchwara shorwa	broth with meat-balls coated with dough
paláw	rice made with meat and carrots
shashlik	barbequed meat (usually mutton) or liver
laghmán	long noodles with fried meat and vegetable soup
manti	steamed big meat-balls coated with dough
sámsa	small pastry

G. Deserts

cake	**pirodzne**	ice-cream	**muz-qaymáq**
cacao	**kakao**	sponge	**biskvit pirodzne**
jam	**murabbá**	jelly	**dzele**

H. Model Dialog

Waiter:	What would you like to have?	**Nima kháhlaysiz?**
Mr. A:	What Uzbek food do you have?	**Qanday Ozbek táamlaringiz bár?**
Waiter:	We have rice, chuchwara and manti.	**Paláw, chuchwara va manti bár.**
Mr. A:	I'll have some rice.	**Men paláwdan álaman.**
Mr. B:	What type of meat dishes do you have?	**Goshtli áwqatlardan nima bár?**
Waiter:	Kabob, steak.	**Kabáb, bifshteks.**
Mr. B:	Please bring me some kabob.	**Marhamat, menga kabáb keltiring.**
Waiter:	What would you like to drink?	**Nima ichishni kháhlaysiz?**
Mr. A:	What drinks do you have?	**Qanday ichimliklaringiz bár.**
Waiter:	We have hot tea and coffee. We don't have milk.	**Issiq cháy va kofemiz bár. Sutimiz yoq.**
Mr. A:	Bring me a glass of water.	**Menga bir stakan su álib keling.**
Mr. B:	I'd like a bottle of wine.	**Bir shisha vina kháhlayman.**
Waiter:	Good appetite!	**Ásh bolsin.**
Mr. A:	Would you bring us some coffee please?	**Bizga qahwa keltirasizmi?**
Waiter:	Would you like some desert?	**Shirinlik kháhlaysizmi?**
Mr. A:	I don't want (any).	**Men kháhlamayman.**

| *Mr. B:* | I don't want any either. | **Men ham kháhlamayman.** |
| *Mr. A:* | Waiter, the check please. | **Ofitsant, lutfan hisáblash sangiz.** |

Food is served in restaurants, cafes, and food stands. Restaurants offer the greatest variety of foods and superior service. Most waiters and waitresses speak Russian in addition to Uzbek.

Chapter 11.   Accommodation

A. Vocabulary

bathroom	**vanna**	room	**khána**
bed	**karavát**	soap	**sáwun**
chair	**stul**	table	**stol**
cold water	**sáwuq su**	telephone	**telefon**
hot water	**issiq su**	television	**televizir**
hotel	**mehmánkhána**	toilet	**tualet**

B. Key Questions and Phrases

I am looking for a good hotel.	**Yakhshi bir mehmánkhána izlayapman.**
Do you have a vacancy?	**Sizda bosh khánalar bármi?**
I need a room for <u>one person.</u>	**Menga <u>bir kishilik</u> khána kerak**
two people	**ikki kishilik**
three people	**uch kishilik**
Is there a <u>bathroom</u> in the room?	**Bu khánada <u>vanna</u> bármi?**
hot water	**issiq su**
telephone	**telefon**
television	**televizir**

Yes, there is.	Ha, bár
No, there isn't.	Yoq.
How many days will you stay?	Necha kun qálasiz?
(I'll stay) <u>one day</u>.	<u>Bir kun</u> (bolaman).
two days	ikki kun
until Saturday	shanbagacha
How much is the room?	Bu khánaning bahási qancha?
I'll take the room.	Men bu khánani álaman.
Do you have a cheaper room?	Arzánráq khánangiz bármi?
Here is your key.	Mana, khánangizning kaliti.
Where is the elevator?	Lift qayerda?
Which floor is my room on?	Khánam nechanchi qawatta?
Where may I make a phone call?	Qayerdan telefon qilishim mumkin?
Where is the <u>restaurant</u>?	<u>Restoran</u> qayerda jáylashgan?
cafeteria	kafe
barber	sartaráshkhána
There is no <u>towel</u> in my room.	Khánamda <u>sáchiq</u> yoq.
hot water	issiq su
soap	sáwun
Which floor is room 53 on?	53 nomerli khána qaysi qawatta?
I will be leaving <u>in the morning.</u>	Men <u>ertalab</u> ketaman.
at two o'clock	sáat ikkida
in the afternoon	tushdan keyin
Please bring me the bill.	Marhamat, menga hisáb-kitábni keltiring.
Call me a taxi please.	Marhamat, taksi chaqirib bering.

Every large city has some good hotels, but book your room in advance,
especially in high season. Most of the good hotels have a bar, a restau-
rant, and live music. Rooms in these hotels have hot running water and
a telephone. Some rooms also have television. Until recently all hotels
were state owned, but now foreign companies are building hotels in
Tashkent, Bukhara and Samarkand.

C. Model Dialog

Do you have a vacancy?	**Bosh khánangiz bármi?**
I need a room for one person.	**Menga bir kishilik khána kerak.**
How many days will you stay?	**Necha kun qálasiz?**
Five days.	**Besh kun.**
I need a room with a shower	**Menga dushli khána kerak.**
We have a room with a shower.	**Dushli khánamiz bár.**
Would you like to see it?	**Korishni kháhlaysizmi?**
That would be nice	**Yakhshi bolardi.**
It is very nice, I'll take it.	**Juda yakhshi. Shu khánani álaman.**
Your passport please.	**Pasportingizni bering.**
Here is my passport	**Marhamat, mana pasportim.**
Here is your key.	**Mana, kalitingiz.**
Room number 23. It is on the 2nd floor.	**Yigirma uchunci (23) khána. Ikkinchi qawatta.**
Thank you. Do you have a restaurant?	**Rahmat. restoraningiz bármi?**
Yes, we do. On the fourth floor.	**Ha, bár. Tortinchi qawatta**

D. Supplementary Vocabulary

baggage	**yuk**	blanket	**adyál**
to call	**chaqir-**	cupboard	**jawán**
form	**blanka**	hotel director	**mehmánkhána ma'muri**
to iron	**dazmálla-**	mattress	**toshak**
mirror	**áyna**	number	**nomer**
passport	**pasport**	pillow	**yástiq**
pillow cover	**yástiq jildi**	refrigerator	**muzlatghich**
to reserve	**buyurtma ber-**	sheets	**cháyshap**
shower	**dush**	taxi	**taksi**
towel	**sáchiq**	to wake up	**uyghát-**

Chapter 12.   Money Matters

A. Key Vocabulary

bank	**bank**	money	**pul**
check	**chek**	coins	**tanga**
dollar	**dollir**	ruble	**som**
to pay	**tola-**	to sign	**qol qoy-**
small change	**mayda pul**	to send	**yubár-**
cash	**naqd pul**	interest	**fáiz**
cashier	**kassir**	cashier's window	**kassa**
amount	**miqdár**	foreign currency	**valyuta**
exchange rate	**kurs**	traveller's check	**sayáhat cheki**
value	**bahá**	to exchange money	**almashtir-**

B. Key Phrases and Questions

Where can I change money?	**Pulni qayerda almashtirish mumkin?**
Where is the foreign currency exchange?	**Valyuta almashtirish bolumi qayerda?**

I want to change some <u>money</u>.
    dollars
	Men <u>pul</u> almashtirmáqchiman.
	    dollir

What is the exchange rate for the <u>frank</u>?
    mark
	<u>Frankning</u> kursi qanday?
	    Markning

How much do you want to exchange?	**Necha dollar almashtirmáqchisiz?**
Are traveller's checks sold here?	**Bu yerda sayáhat chekleri sátiladimi?**
I want to send some money to the US.	**AQSh'ga pul yubármáqchiman.**
May I see your passport?	**Pasportingizni korish mumkinmi?**
Could you please sign here?	**Marhamat, bu yerga qol qoyasizmi?**

Credit cards are rarely used. Most establishments do business in cash. One can change money at foreign exchange offices in large hotels or in banks. The basic monetary unit is the Russian ruble which in Uzbekistan is called a som. In the 90's due to the devaluation of the ruble, the 'tiyin,' the equivalent of the Russian kopeck, went out of use .

Chapter 13.   At the Post Office

A. Vocabulary

air mail	**aviyapochta**	letter	**khat**
form	**blanka**	envelope	**kanvert**
parcel	**pasilka**	postage stamp	**marka**
post card	**atkritka**	post office	**pochta telegraf**
registered	**buyurtma**	receipt	**kvitantsiya**
sender	**jonatuwchi**	telegram	**telegramma**
telephone	**telefon**	to phone	**telefon qil-**
address	**adres**	addressee	**áluwchi**
phone number	**telefon nomeri**	phone booth	**telefon budkasi**

B. At the Post Office

parcel	**pasilkani**
I want to send this <u>letter</u> to <u>Moscow</u>.	**Men bu <u>khatni</u> <u>Maskvaga</u> yubár máqchiman.**
the US	**AQSh'ga**
What does it cost by airmail?	**Aviyapochta árqali qancha turadi?**

How many <u>stamps</u> do you need?	Sizga qancha <u>marka</u> kerak?
envelopes	kanvert
Give me two <u>envelopes</u>.	Menga ikkita <u>kanvert</u> bering.
stamps	marka
postcards	atkritka
Here are your <u>envelopes</u>.	Mana <u>kanvertlaringiz</u>.
stamps	markalaringiz
How much a <u>letter</u> to the US ?	AQSh'ga yubáriladigan <u>khat</u> qancha turadi?
parcel	pasilka
Can I send these books by parcel-post?	Bu kitáblarni pasilka bilanjonatishim mumk inmi?
What are the contents of this parcel?	Bu pasilkaning ichida nima bár?
Please fill in this form.	Marhamat, bu blankani tolghazing.
How much does my telegram cost?	Mening telegrammam necha pul turadi?

C. On the Phone

I want to make a telephone call to <u>London</u>.	Men <u>Londinga</u> telefon qilmáqchiman.
New York	Niy-York
I want to book a call to <u>Istanbul</u>.	Men <u>Istanbul</u> bilan gaplashishni buyurt máqchiman
Washington	Washington
My telephone number is...	Mening telefon nomerim....
Give me your phone number please?	Marhamat nomeringizni bering.
Is there a phone booth here?	Bu yerda telefon budkasi bármi?
This telephone is <u>out of order</u>.	Bu telefon <u>buzuq</u>.
working	ishlaydi
I need a phone book.	Menga telefon ma'lumátnámasi kerak.
The line is busy.	Liniya bosh emas.
Which number should I dial?	Qaysi raqamni teray?
There is a call for you.	Sizni telefonda sorashyapti.
The number that you are calling is not answering.	Siz qongiráq qilgan nomer javáb bermayapti.

May I speak to Ms. Gulbahar?	**Men gulbahár khánim bilan gaplasha álamanmi?**
This is Bill speaking.	**Bill gapiryapti.**
What is the charge per minute?	**Bir minut gaplashish necha pul turadi?**

D. Model Dialog

I'd like to send an <u>ordinary</u> telegram.	**Men <u>áddiy</u> telegramma jonatmáqchiman.**
express	**sháshilinch**
Where to?	**Qayerga?**
To England. What is the rate per word?	**Angliyaga. Bitta soz necha pul turadi?**
The rate per word is 15 rubles.	**Bitta soz on besh som turadi.**
Is there any charge for the address?	**Adres uchun pul tolash kerakmi?**
No there isn't.	**Kerak emas.**
How much does my telegram cost?	**Mening telegrammam necha pul turadi?**
235 rubles.	**Ikki yuz ottiz besh (235) som turadi.**

The communication system in Uzbekistan is better than in many developing countries but inferior to that in Europe and the U.S. There are public phones on busy street corners and almost all offices, but only a few homes have phones. To make a long distance call, it is advisable to go to a major hotel. Mail service from Uzbekistan usually takes much longer than from other comparable areas. One can find all the postal services such as telegram, phone, and parcel post, but they are relatively slow. Fax is just being introduced and is available in only a very few places.

E. Supplementary Vocabulary

express	**sháshilinch**	to speak on the phone	**telefonda sozlash-**
mail box	**pochta qutisi**	money order	**pul jonatmasi**
receiver	**trubka**	to dial	**raqam ter-**
long distances	**haharlarará**	hello	**allo, labbay**
parcel section	**pasilka bolimi**	public phone	**telefon-aftamat**
domestic letter	**yurt ichi khat**		

Chapter 14.   Shopping

A. Vocabulary

market	**bázár**	shop	**dokán**
customer	**kharidár**	department store	**univermag**
store	**magazin**	clothing store	**kiyim dokáni**
price	**narkh, bahá**	book store	**kitáb magazini**
to buy	**sátib ál-**	to go shopping	**kharid qilish**
cheap	**arzán**	expensive	**qimmat**
scale	**tarázi**	cashier	**kassa**
department	**bolim**	salesperson	**sátuwchi**

B. Key Phrases and Questions

When does the shop open?	**Dokán qachán áchiladi?**
close	**yápiladi**
I want to buy a skirt.	**Men yubka sátib álmáqchiman.**
tooth paste	**tish pastasi**
tooth brush	**miswák**
handkerchief	**dastromál**
How much is it?	**Bu necha pul turadi?**
How much is this blouse?	**Bu bluza necha pul turadi?**
shirt	**koylak**
hat	**shlyapa**
are these pants	**shim**
socks	**paypáq**
This is too expensive.	**Bu juda qimmat.**
Can you lower the price?	**Narkhini tushura álasizmi?**
Yes, we can.	**Ha, tushura álaman.**
No, we can't.	**Yoq, tushura álmayman.**
Is there a cheaper one?	**Arzánrághi bármi?**
bigger	**kattarághi**
smaller	**kichikrághi**
Do you have a sweater?	**Sizda sviter bármi?**
scarf	**bojinbágh**
raincoat	**plash**
Which raincoat do you want?	**Qaysi plashni kháhlaysiz?**
like	**yakhshi korasiz.**
I want the black raincoat.	**Men qára plashni kháhlayman.**
white	**áq**
brown	**qahwarang**
red	**qirmizi**
blue	**máwi**
green	**yashil**
yellow	**sariq**
Show me that silk shirt.	**Menga u ipak koylakni korsating.**
I liked this one.	**Bu menga yáqdi.**
I didn't like this one.	**Bu menga yáqmadi.**
I'll buy this one.	**Men buni álaman.**

C. Model Dialog

Is there a book store around here?	**Yaqin atráfda kitáb magazini bármi?**
Yes, it is next to the bus-stop.	**Ha, u aftobus bekatining yánida.**
Where are the foreign language books sold?	**Khárijiy tildaki kitáblar qayerda sátiladi?**
On the second floor.	**Ikkinci qawatta sátiladi.**
Do you have an English-Uzbek Dictionary?	**Sizda Ingilizcha-Ozbekcha lughat bármi?**
Yes, we have the new edition.	**Ha, bizda yangi nashri bár.**
How much is it?	**Necha pul turadi?**
Twenty-seven rubles.	**Yigirma yetti som.**

There are several state owned department stores in the big cities. Private stores and shops began to appear after independence, and their number is gradually increasing. Uzbek (open) markets, known as bazaars, are cheap and very colorful. One can find all kinds of food there. The goods are usually very fresh. Bargaining is very common except in department stores. One can find good silk cloth, leather goods, china tea pots, copper trays and souvenirs.

D. Supplementary Vocabulary

fabric	**gazlama**	size	**razmer**
color	**rang**	clothes	**kiyim**
big/loose	**keng**	tight	**tár**
long	**uzun**	short	**qisqa**
shoes	**áyáq kiyimi**	comb	**taráq**
perfume	**atir**	clothing	**kiyim**
satin	**atlas**	belt	**belbágh**
to put on	**kiy-**	womens	**ayállar**
mens	**erkaklar**	childrens	**bálalar**

Chapter 15.   Weather

A. Vocabulary

weather	**áb-hawá, hawá**	climate	**iqlim, áb-u hawá**
air	**hawá**	hot	**issiq**
cold	**sáwuq**	cool	**salqin**
warm	**iliq**	thermometer	**termometr**
cloud	**bulut**	cloudy	**bulutli**
rain	**yámghir**	rainy	**yámghirli**
snow	**qár**	snowy	**qár, qárli**
sun	**quyásh**	sunny	**quyáshli, áchiq**
wind	**shamál**	windy	**shamálli**
storm	**borán**	stormy	**boránli**
temperature	**harárat, hawá harárati**	degree	**daraja, gradus**
lightning	**yashin**	thunder	**mámaqaldiráq**
mist, fog	**tuman**	weather report	**áb-hawá ma'lumáti**

B. Key Phrases and Questions

What's the weather like <u>today</u>? **<u>Bugun</u> áb-hawá qanday?**
   now **házir**
The weather is <u>nice</u> today. **Bugun hawá <u>yakhshi</u>.**
   hot **issiq**
What's the temperature <u>today</u>? **<u>Bugun</u> harárat qanday?**
   now **házir**
It is <u>+10 C</u> now. **Házir <u>on daraja issiq</u>**
   -3 C **uch daraja sáwuq**
What will the weather be like <u>today</u>? **<u>Bugun</u> hawá qanday boladi?**
   tomorrow **ertaga**
   next week **kelasi hafta**
It will <u>rain</u> tomorrow. **Ertaga <u>yámghir</u> yághadi.**
   snow **qár**

It will be <u>rainy</u> tomorrow.	**Ertaga <u>yámghirli</u> boladi**
mild	**yumsháq**
foggy	**tumanli**
What splendid weather!	**Qanday ajáyib hawá!**

C. Model Dialog

What will the weather be like tomorrow?	**Ertaga áb-hawá qanday boladi?**
It will snow tomorrow.	**Ertaga qár yághadi.**
What will be the road conditions?	**Yollarning ahwáli qanday boladi?**
Some roads will be open, and some closed.	**Ba'zi yollar áchiq, ba'zi yollar yápiq.**
What 's the temperature now?	**Házir hawáning harárati necha daraja?**
It is + 4 C right now.	**Házir tort daraja issiq.**
I like this kind of weather.	**Menga shunaqa hawá yáqadi.**

Uzbekistan is usually cold in winter and hot in summer. The best time to visit Uzbekistan is in the late spring and early fall. Temperature changes may occur between day and night.

D. Supplementary Vocabulary

to blow	**es-**	to melt	**eri-**
drizzle	**mayda yámghir**	hail	**dol**
ice	**muz**	frozen	**muzlagan**
sunrise	**quyásh chiqishi**	sunset	**quyásh bátishi**
overcast	**dim**	mild	**yumsháq**
bad	**yámán**	slippery	**sirghanchik**
barometer	**barometr**	heat	**issiqliq**
flood	**su táshqini**	drought	**qurgháqchilik**

sky	**ásmán**	star	**yulduz**
season	**mawsum**	to fall (of rain etc.)	**yágh-**
winter	**qish**	spring	**bahár**
summer	**yáz**	fall	**kuz**

Drills

In this section we will do pronunciation and repetition drills with some of the most frequently used key questions, answers and phrases. All of them were introduced in preceding chapters.

Personal Information

What is your name?	**Ismingiz nima?**
My name is...	**Ismim ...**
What is your surname?	**Familiyangiz nima?**
My surname is...	**Familiyam ...**
How old are you?	**Yáshingiz nechada?**
I am 25 years old.	**Men (25) yigirma besh yáshdaman.**
Are you married? (for a man only)	**Siz uylanganmisiz?**
Yes, I'm married.	**Ha, men uylanganman.**
No, I'm not married.	**Yoq, men uylanmaganman.**
Are you married? (for a woman only)	**Siz turmushga chiqqanmisiz?**
Yes, I'm married.	**Ha, men turmushga chiqqanman.**
No, I'm not married.	**Yoq, men turmushga chiqmaganman.**
What is your nationality?	**Millatingiz nima?**
I'm an American.	**Men amerikalikman.**
What is your occupation?	**Kasbingiz nima?**
I'm an engineer.	**Men endzenerman.**
I'm a doctor.	**Men doktirman.**

Do you have ...?

Do you have money?	**Pulingiz bármi?**
Do you have a <u>passport</u>?	<u>**Pasportingiz**</u> **bármi?**
ticket	**bilet**
pen	**ruchka**
Do you have a cheaper room?	**Arzánráq khánangiz bármi?**
Do you have a vacancy?	**Sizda bosh khánalar bármi?**

Do you have a <u>sweater</u>?	**Sizda <u>sviter</u> bármi?**
scarf	**boyinbágh**
raincoat	**plash**
I have <u>money</u>.	**Pulim bár.**
a pen.	**ruchka**
a ticket	**bilet**
I don't have money.	**Pulim yoq.**
I don't have <u>a pen</u>.	**<u>Ruchkam</u> yoq.**
a ticket	**bilet**

Is there a ...?

Is there a <u>bank</u> near here?	**Bu atráfd a <u>bank</u> bármi?**
doctor	**doktir**
hospital	**kasalkhána**
hotel	**mehmánkhána**
pharmacy	**dárikhána**
restaurant	**restoran**
subway station	**metro stantsiyasi**
Is there a <u>plane</u> to Tashkent?	**Táshkenga <u>samalyot</u> bármi?**
train	**poyezd**
Is there a <u>bathroom</u> in the room?	**Bu khánada <u>vanna</u> bármi?**
hot water	**issiq su**
telephone	**telefon**
television	**televizir**
Is there a <u>cheaper</u> one?	**<u>Arzánrághi</u> bármi?**
bigger	**kattarághi**
smaller	**kichikrághi**
Yes, there is.	**Ha, bár**
No, there isn't.	**Yoq.**
There is no <u>towel</u> in my room.	**Khánamda <u>sáchiq</u> yoq.**
hot water	**issiq su**
soap	**sáwun**

Where is ...?

Where is the <u>police station</u>?	**<u>Militsiya idárasi</u> qayerda?**
cinema	**kinateatr**
museum	**muzey**
American Embassy	**Amerikan konsulkhánasi**

post office	**pochta**
railway station	**vagzal**
zoo	**haywánát bághi**
Where is the information?	**Sprafka byurosi qayerda?**
Where is the elevator?	**Lift qayerda?**
Where is the <u>restaurant</u>?	<u>**Restoran**</u> **qayerda jáylashgan?**
cafeteria	**kafe**
barber	**sartaráshkhána**
Where is the nearest <u>bank</u>?	**Eng yaqin <u>bank</u> qayerda?**
bus-stop	**aftobus bekati**
hotel	**mehmánkhána**
How does one get to the <u>Navai Museum</u>?	<u>**Nawáiy muzeyiga**</u> **qanday báriladi?**
to the airport	**ayeroportga**
to the Uzbekiston Hotel	**Ozbekistán mehmánkhánasiga**
to Farabi Street	**Fárábiy kochasiga**

I need/want ...?

I need a taxi.	**Menga taksi kerak.**
I need a ticket to Moscow.	**Menga Maskvaga bilet kerak.**
I need a room for <u>one person</u>.	**Menga <u>bir kishilik</u> khána kerak**
two people	**ikki kishilik**
I need a phone book.	**Menga telefon ma'lumátná masi kerak.**
Give me two <u>envelopes</u>.	**Menga ikkita <u>kanvert</u> bering.**
stamps	**marka**
postcards	**atkritka**
Give me your phone number.	**Menga telefon nomeringizni bering.**
Show me that silk <u>shirt</u>.	**Menga u ipak <u>koylakni</u> korsating.**
tie	**galstukni**
Where would you like to go?	**Qayerga bármáqchisiz?**
I want to got to <u>Pushkin Street</u>.	<u>**Pushkin kochasiga**</u> **ketmáqchiman.**
to Tashkent Hotel.	**Táshkent mehmánkhánasiga**
I want to buy a <u>skirt</u>.	**Men <u>yubka</u> sátib álmáqchiman.**
tooth paste	**tish pastasi**
tooth brush	**miswák**
handkerchief	**dastromál**
I want the black raincoat.	**Men qára plashni kháhlayman.**
I liked this one.	**Bu menga yáqdi.**
I liked the big teapot.	**Katta cháynak menga yáqdi.**

I didn't like this one.	**Bu menga yáqmadi.**
I didn't like this coffee.	**Bu kafe menga yáqmadi.**
What would you like to <u>eat</u>?	**Nima <u>yeyishni</u> kháhlaysiz?**
to drink	**ichishni**
to read	**oqishni**
to buy	**sátib álishni**
I'd like <u>coffee</u>.	**Men <u>kofe</u> kháhlayman.**
two bottles of beer	**ikki shisha piwá**
a cup of tea	**bir piyála cháy**
I want to make a telephone call <u>to London</u>.	**Men <u>Londinga telefon</u> qilmáqchiman.**
to New York	**Niy-Yorkga**
Would you like fish or chicken?	**Siz baliqmi yeysiz yá táwuqmi yeysiz?**
I'd like some fish.	**Men baliq istayman.**
I do not want <u>chicken</u>.	**Men <u>táwuq</u> istamayman.**
anything	**hech narsa**
Would you like some <u>fish</u>?	**<u>Baliq</u> istaysizmi?**
chicken	**táwuq**
Would you like some <u>sugar</u>?	**Siz <u>qand</u> kháhlaysizmi?**
milk	**sut**
salt	**tuz**
pepper	**murch**
bread	**nán**
Yes, please.	**Ha, marhamat.**
No, thank you.	**Yoq, rahmat.**

How much is ...?

How much is this?	**Bu necha pul turadi?**
How much is the <u>ticket</u>?	**<u>Bilet</u> necha pul turadi?**
book	**kitáb**
tea	**cháy**
watermelon	**tarwuz**
How much is the room?	**Bu khánaning bahási qancha?**
How much does my telegram cost?	**Mening telegrammam necha pul turadi?**
How much is <u>this blouse</u>?	**Bu <u>bluza</u> necha pul turadi?**
shirt	**koylak**
hat	**shlyapa**

Numbers

1	bir	11	on bir	30	ottiz
2	ikki	12	on ikki	40	qirq
3	uch	13	on uch	50	ellik
4	tort	14	on tort	60	áltmish
5	besh	15	on besh	70	yetmish
6	álti	16	on álti	80	saksán
7	yetti	17	on yetti	90	toqsán
8	sakkiz	18	on sakkiz		
9	toqqiz	19	on toqqiz		
10	on	20	yigirma		

100s
100	bir yuz
200	ikki yuz
300	uch yuz
400	tort yuz
500	besh yuz
600	álti yuz
700	yetti yuz
800	sakkiz yuz
900	toqqiz yuz

1000s
1,000	bir ming
2,000	ikki ming
3,000	uch ming
4,000	tort ming
10,000	on ming
42,000	qirq ikki ming
700,000	yetti yuz ming

1,000,000s
1,000,000	bir milyon
2,000,000	ikki milyon
50,000,000	ellik milyon

1st, 2nd etc.
1st	birinchi
2nd	ikkinchi
3rd	uchinchi
4th	tortinchi
5th	beshinchi

Days
Monday	dushanba	Friday	juma
Tuesday	seshanba	Saturday	shanba
Wednesday	chárshanba	Sunday	yakshanba
Thursday	payshanba		

Months
January	yanvar	July	iyul
February	fevral	August	awgust
March	mart	September	sentyabr
April	aprel	October	aktyabr
May	may	November	nayabr
June	iyun	December	dekabr

Personal Pronouns

I	**men**	we	**biz**
you	**sen**	you	**siz**
he, she, it	**u**	they	**ular**

Verb Suffixes

men bilaman	I know	**biz bilamiz**	we know
sen bilasan	you know	**siz bilasiz**	you know
u biladi	he, she, it knows	**ular biladi(lar)**	they know

I know	**Bilaman**	I don't know	**Bilmayman**
I understand	**Tushunaman**	I don't understand	**Tushunmayman**
I want (it)	**Istayman, kháhlayman**		
I don't want (it)	**Istamayman, kháhlamayman**		

I'm an American.	**Men amerikalikman.**
I'm an engineer.	**Men endzenyerman.**
I'm a doctor.	**Men doktirman.**
I am sick.	**Men kasalman.**
I am pregnant.	**Hámiladárman.**
Goodbye	**Khayr**